First Steps in Theology

Bob Gordon

with

David Fardouly

Sovereign World

© 1988 Bob Gordon

Sovereign World Ltd
PO Box 17
Chichester
West Sussex
PO20 6RY
England

Unless otherwise stated, all Scripture quotations are from the New
International Version, © 1973, 1978 International Bible Society.
Published by Hodder & Stoughton.

ISBN 1 85240 27 7

CONTENTS

Introduction

The best way to do this course is with the help of an appointed person from a local church. It is suggested that you first go through each study on your own and then with the appointed person so that they can help you to understand what you have read and answer your questions. They will be there to help you and be a friend to you at the beginning of your Christian life. It is also possible to do this study course as part of a small group or on your own.

As you do the course expect God to speak to you and tell you more about Himself. Pray (or talk) with God before you begin each study. Ask His help to understand what you are reading and look for things you need to apply to your life. Do not hurry through the studies. If you are doing them with another person then work out times that are mutually convenient to meet and set your pace together. A group will set its own times. If you are doing the studies alone then do not attempt more than one study per day (the exception to this is study 1 and 2 which may be done together).

The Bible references are written in short-hand, e.g. —

1	John	2	:	3
Number of the		Chapter	Verse	
Book (if applicable)	Book Name	Number	Number	

If more than one verse is referred to, read from the first verse mentioned through to the last one, e.g.—1-3 means read verses 1,2 and 3.

Most Bibles have a contents page at or near the front to which you can refer in order to obtain the page number for the book mentioned. The Bible verses quoted are from the New International Version of the Bible unless otherwise stated.

Note: If there is a word in the booklet that you do not understand, check the Glossary at the back of this booklet.

Study 1

The Work Of Jesus

Who was Jesus?

— If Jesus was who He claimed to be, then He was the most important person that ever lived. He claimed to be the Son of God, the Creator and Supreme ruler of the universe, who came into the world to rescue all mankind.

— If Jesus wasn't who he claimed to be then He must have either been mad or a confidence man. That would mean that millions of people throughout history have been fooled and even given up their lives for a lie. However, history itself has been changed by this man and about one-third of the world's population today at least nominally follow Him. Millions of people claim to know Him personally and they live their lives under His guidance and direction. If He was a liar or a lunatic, He made quite an impact!

— If Jesus is who He claims and He did die, was resurrected and went to be with His Father in heaven, then He is alive today and we ignore Him at our peril.

Could He be the vital ingredient your life is missing?

Is He the piece of jigsaw that makes all the other pieces make sense?

What did Jesus do for us?

He came to:—

1) *Deliver us from Judgement*

> *"Man is destined to die once, and after that to face judgement."*   (Hebrews 9:27)

Physical death is not the greatest threat to a person. Death in a spiritual sense is a more horrific prospect. This means absolute and eternal separation from a loving God. God's judgement of spiritual death is a consequence of our sin. However, Jesus carried our sins and took the judgement on Himself so that those who trust in Him need fear no judgement.

2) *To show us the love of God*

> *"This is love: not that we loved God, but that he loved us and sent his Son as an atoning sacrifice for our sins."*
>   (I John 4:10)

The love of God for every one of us is beyond human understanding. This is not mere friendship, affection or loyalty. Not even the deepest love between two human beings. It is 'agape', the sacrificial love of God who gives Himself completely to save His creation, man.

3) *To make forgiveness possible*

> *"In him we have redemption through his blood, the forgiveness of sins."*   (Ephesians 1:7)

Guilt is the universal problem of the human race. Often we feel guilty but don't know what we feel guilty about. The truth is that our sin has separated us from God and disrupted our consciences and this is the cause of our feelings of guilt. Jesus, however, carried that guilt on our behalf and by putting our trust in Jesus we can be forgiven for all that we have done to displease God. Then we will no longer be separated from God and we will be free from guilt.

4) *To bring us back to God*

"Christ died for sins once for all, the righteous for the unrighteous, to bring you to God."

(I Peter 3:18)

Man is a stranger, lost on his own planet. His rebellion and pride have separated him from his Maker. He has lost his home and his way back home. Jesus came to save the lost and through His death He has made the way back to God.

5) *To release the healing power of God*

"He himself bore our sins in his body on the tree...by his wounds you have been healed." (I Peter 2:24)

Sickness and pain were never part of God's original plan for man. They are not part of His future plan either (see Revelation 21:4). Today you can know the healing and delivering power of God. On the Cross Jesus entered into our suffering and pain and rescued us from both the power and the effects of sin and sickness.

6) *To overcome the powers of evil*

"Having disarmed the powers and authorities, he made a public spectacle of them, triumphing over them by the cross." (Colossians 2:15)

The powers of darkness threaten to engulf mankind. Satan (the devil) is the prince of darkness and he tries to keep people blind as far as God is concerned. But on the Cross, Jesus confronted every power of evil and Satan himself and through His death and resurrection He overthrew them completely.

7) *To rescue us from death*

> *"That by his death he might destroy him who holds the power of death—that is, the devil—and free those who all their lives were held in slavery by their fear of death."*
> (Hebrews 2:14,15)

'Death is a terrible thing for it is an end', said Aristotle the philosopher. But the 'grim reaper' holds no fear for the Christian because his trust is in Jesus who went into death and broke its power completely through the power of His resurrection.

8) *To give us resurrection power*

> *"If we have been united with him in his death, we will certainly also be united with him in his resurrection."*
> (Romans 6:5)

This does not mean that we have to wait until after we die to experience the resurrection power of God. We can know it now! Apart from God's power we are spiritual weaklings. We have not the ability to handle ourselves let alone the situation we find ourselves in every day. God wants to put into our lives the same power by which He raised Jesus from the dead. (see Ephesians 1:18-23)

Prayer:

Almighty God, Jesus seems to have done so much for me. If Jesus really is the Son of God and the Saviour of the world then I do want to know Him personally. Open my eyes and show me the truth. I ask this in Jesus' name. Amen.

Study 2

For God So Loved The World

God's Plan

"For God so loved the world (that includes you!) that he gave his one and only Son, that whoever believes in him shall not perish but have eternal life."   (John 3:16)

God created a beautiful world, and it is His plan that man would serve and worship God. However, this plan has been spoiled by everyone from the first man until you and me. We have all rebelled against God, choosing to live as we want to, without Him. The Bible calls this sin. Because of this the human race has become spoiled bringing chaos and disaster to the world.

God's Son

"For all have sinned and fall short of the glory of God."
(Romans 3:23)

We deserve to suffer the consequence of our sin and rejection of God, which is to be rejected by God forever. However, God loves the world, you and me, so much that He sent His Son Jesus, who was also God, to share our life and hardships. But unlike us, Jesus did not sin. In fact, He went about reversing the effects of our rebellion. God's anger for our rebellion fell on Jesus, who was perfectly innocent. He was punished instead of us and died an agonising death. The Bible says that when He was crucified He took our sinfulness into Himself. Jesus did not stay dead though. God raised Him from the dead and He appeared to many on earth before God took Him up to be with Himself. Jesus' life, death and resurrection opened up the way for us to have a restored relationship with God.

God's Forgiveness

"He who conceals his sin does not prosper, but whoever confesses and renounces them finds mercy."

(Proverbs 28:13)

Before we are made right with God, we need to say we are sorry for our rebellion, admit that we are wrong and ask for God's forgiveness, believing that Jesus died in our place. When God forgives us, we are made right with Him and we can begin our lives again. It is really like being born again into a new life because God sees us as new. God even gives us the Holy Spirit, who is also God, to help us live the life that He wants for us.

God's Answer

Jesus said, "I am the way and the truth and the life. No-one comes to the Father except through me."

(John 14:6)

Man has tried all sorts of things to restore his inner need to have a relationship with God including good works, charity and religion. These things fail to achieve their goal because they are not God's answer to the problem of our separation from Him. God's answer is JESUS.

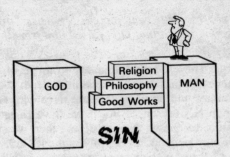

Man's Problem — Separation

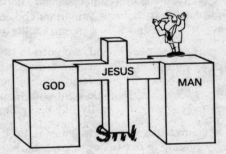

God's Solution — The Cross

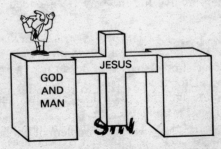

Man's Response — Receiving Christ

Our Choice

"If you confess with your mouth, 'Jesus is Lord', and believe in your heart that God raised him from the dead, you will be saved."   (Romans 10:9)

Jesus said that He will return one day to judge the world, both the ones alive and the ones who have died. When this happens the ones who have been made right with God will live forever in His presence. But if we have rejected God and His plan to rescue us through Jesus, then we still face the result of our decision: an eternity without God, without love, without friends, without hope and without anything good or beautiful. God has given us a choice; we must choose today before it is too late. It is the most important choice that we will ever have to make and it is a matter of life or death.

Life to the Full

Jesus said, "I have come that they may have life, and have it to the full."   (John 10:10)

God wants to change this world. He wants to do it through you and me by coming to live in our hearts, sharing our problems, our joys, our difficulties and sharing His Holy Spirit power to help us live life the way He intended.

Our Response

There are four simple steps in order to take a hold of the work Jesus did for us:—

1. We need to admit that we do displease God (sin) and fall short of God's standard.
2. We need, with God's help, to turn from going our own way and go God's way instead (repentance).

3. We need to believe that Jesus Christ, God's Son, died on the Cross to take the punishment for our sin and therefore enabled us to have a relationship with God again.
4. We need to believe that God raised Jesus from the dead and that He is now at the right hand of God the Father. We need to trust Jesus and make Him our Lord and Saviour and commit our lives to Him. To make someone Lord means we make them the boss. When Jesus asks us to do something we need to obey Him.

God's Assurance

If you pray the prayer at the end of this study (or you have prayed another like it) and you prayed it from your heart, meaning every word, then you are a Christian. Whether you felt anything or not you are changed because God has promised this and He cannot lie. You have become a disciple or follower of Jesus. The step you have made is only the beginning. It is like being born again and starting a new life. You are now a child of God and He has given you the Holy Spirit so that you will have all the help and power you need to live a life pleasing to God. Just as a new-born baby has many needs in order to grow and mature, so does a new Christian. Read and study the rest of this booklet to discover some of the basic things God wants you to do now you are a Christian.

Questions and Tips:

1. What do the following verses say about why God sent His Son Jesus into the world? (John 3:16-18; John 17:2)
2. What is the consequence of displeasing God (sinning)? (Isaiah 59:2)
3. What do we need to do? (Mark 1:15; Acts 3:19)

4. Forgiveness means to remove and forget. Read I John 1:9 in the light of this.
5. What will we do if we love God? (John 14:23)
6. Do we really receive the Holy Spirit when we become a Christian? (Ephesians 1:13,14)
7. Read the following verses for your encouragement: John 1:12; John 5:24; Romans 5:8; Hebrews 13:5; I John 5:11,12.

Prayer:

Almighty God, it is true that I do things that fall short of your standard. I honestly want to turn from all this that I recognise as sin. I ask your forgiveness for all I have done that is wrong in your sight. I want to go your way instead of my own way. Thank you for sending your Son Jesus to die on the Cross so that I can be free of the punishment I deserve. I am glad that you raised Jesus from the dead and that He is alive today. I make Jesus the Lord of my life. Please come into my life right now so that I may be made new. Thank you for hearing my prayer. Please help me now to live the rest of my life with the help and power of the Holy Spirit that you have given to me. I pray this in Jesus' name. Amen.

Study 3

I'm Going God's Way Now

1. Following Jesus

Every true Christian is called to be a disciple of Jesus. This means they will follow Jesus and put the claims of Jesus first in their life, regardless of the cost to themselves. They will be determined to live a life according to the example Jesus set.

> *"Whoever claims to live in him must walk as Jesus did."*
> (I John 2:6)

As you live more in the light of who God is and what He has said, many questions, tensions, confusions, perplexities and doubts will start to fade. Although some difficult circumstances may remain, you can trust that God is in control and experience real inner peace and joy.

2. Putting God First

> *"Seek first his kingdom and his righteousness, and all these things will be given to you."*   (Matthew 6:33)

God has given us many privileges or benefits as His followers but we also have certain responsibilities. God expects us to thank Him for all He has done for us and obey Him when

He shows us His way. Our going on with Christ and growing as a Christian is conditional upon our obedience to God's will. We need to put God first and live for Him rather than ourselves.

> Jesus said, *'If anyone would come after me, he must deny himself and take up his cross daily and follow me. For whoever wants to save his life will lose it, but whoever loses his life for me will save it.'*   (Luke 9:23,24)

Following Jesus in this way may mean struggle and trials but it also means the privilege of resting in Jesus (read Matthew 11:28-30). As you put Jesus, His will and His work first in your life, you will begin to fully experience God's love and care because He has promised to provide all your daily needs (read Matthew 6:25-34).

> *"I (you) can do everything through him (Jesus) who gives me (you) strength."*   (Philippians 4:13)

We need to dedicate our lives to Jesus and follow and obey Him every day. The standards of life for the real Christian are much higher than the world's standards. It takes courage to follow Jesus in the way He wants but He will give us all the courage and strength we need if we look to Him and do as He requires.

3. God's Way Holds Pleasure and Fulfilment

> *"You have made known to me the path of life; you will fill me with joy in your presence (here on earth), with eternal pleasures at your right hand."*   Psalm 16:11

Being a Christian isn't a bore but rather there is great pleasure and fulfilment in it that nothing else can bring, because Christians are living a life that is pleasing to God. The pleasure of sin will eventually destroy you, but God's pleasures will benefit you for all eternity.

4. God Will Show Us His Way Which Is The Best Way

When you make important decisions as a Christian, don't just do what you feel is right but rather seek God and let His Holy Spirit guide you. Also be influenced by God's Word (the Bible) as you read it daily. If you are not sure what to do or you want God's guidance, a good question to ask yourself is 'What would Jesus do?'. If you have the slightest doubt then don't do it, especially if your God-given conscience is troubling you. Let God guide you and let the peace of God rule in your heart (see Colossians 3:15).

> *"Trust in the Lord with all your heart and lean not on your own understanding; in all your ways acknowledge him, and he will make your paths straight."* (Proverbs 3:5,6)

Seek to put Jesus first in all you do. If you find you cannot invite Jesus into an aspect of your life (perhaps something you are ashamed of), then cut out that activity or area because it will lead you away from God. Let God work out His plan and His will for you. You have trusted Him with your soul for eternity, now trust Him with your daily life. Trust Him to sort out your problems and needs. He *can* and *will* help you in everything.

> *"And my God will meet all your needs according to his glorious riches in Christ Jesus."* (Philippians 4:19)

5. God Asks Us To Live By Faith

"Now faith is being sure of what we hope for and certain of what we do not see." (Hebrews 11:1)

Faith is believing God and what He has said rather than what we see or feel. We need faith in God.

"Without faith it is impossible to please God, because anyone who comes to Him must believe that He exists and that He rewards those who earnestly seek him." (Hebrews 11:6)

6. How Do We Receive Faith?

"So faith comes from hearing and hearing by the word of Christ." (Romans 10:17 New American Standard Version)

Faith comes when we hear God's word to us and we believe that God will do as He says He will. If you have given your life to Jesus and therefore are born again, then you have a measure of faith.

"Therefore, since we have been justified through faith, we have peace with God through our Lord Jesus Christ, through whom we have gained access by faith into this grace in which we now stand. And we rejoice in the hope of the glory of God." (Romans 5:1,2)

7. Can We Express Our Faith In Giving?

God has inexhaustible riches available for His children. We are heirs to all He possesses (see Romans 8:17) and God is

eager to share those riches with us (see Romans 8:32).
Everything we have is from God and He has made us stewards
or caretakers of this. We can show our gratitude to God by
giving generously of ourselves—our time, possessions, talents
and money—to those who have needs. Giving is learning how
to share and be a good steward of what God has given us.
The Bible says,

> *"Remember this: Whoever sows sparingly will also reap
> sparingly and whoever sows generously will also reap
> generously."*   (II Corinthians 9:6)

We cannot give more than God will give back to us
(see Luke 6:38).

Questions and Tips:

1. How should we live as disciples of Jesus according to John
   8:31,32 and Colossians 3:17?
2. Do we have a responsibility before God for the way we
   live? (Matthew 5:16)
3. What do the following verses say about us in Christ Jesus?
   (II Corinthians 5:17; Colossians 2:9,10; 3:9,10)
4. Can anything separate us from the love of God? (Romans
   8:38,39)
5. What assurance that we are children of God does the Holy
   Spirit give us? (Romans 8:14-17)
6. What is the greatest characteristic a believer can manifest?
   (I Corinthians 13:1-13)
7. For your encouragement read: Ephesians 2:6-10; II
   Peter 1:3.
8. Does walking by faith mean we shut our eyes and do what
   we feel is right and hope for the best? (Hebrews 12:2)
9. What can faith in God do? (Mark 11:22,23)

Prayer:

Almighty God, thank you for all you have done for me in Jesus. I want to live as His disciple. Please help me and strengthen me as I seek to do this. Show me what Jesus would do in every situation that I face. Help me always to put Him first in everything that I do. Thank you also for the faith you have given to me that has enabled me to become one of your children. Help my faith to grow that I might serve you more effectively. There is still much that I do not understand but I trust my life into your hands. I ask this in Jesus' name. Amen.

Study 4

Reading God's Word

The need to mature

Now that you have become a Christian, you are a new creation, you are born-again (see II Corinthians 5:17). Spiritually you are like an infant or baby who needs to begin to grow to maturity. The Word of God tells us,

> *"Like new born babies, crave pure spiritual milk, so that by it you may grow up in your salvation."*
>
> (I Peter 2:2)

The milk referred to here is the Word of God (the Bible). We need to read this regularly, meditate on it and obey it. This is basic for Christian growth and maturity. Without it we will stay as spiritual babies and never grow.

What to do

It is important that you get at least a New Testament in a modern translation of the Bible. The easiest to read versions are the 'Good News for Modern Man' or the 'Living Bible'. The translation we recommend however is the 'New International Version'. As Christians we need to set aside time to read God's Word each day. In fact, we shouldn't let a day go by without reading some of the Bible. A good place to start reading is John's gospel in the New Testament. Read at least a chapter a day. Before you start to read pray that God will show you more about Himself and what you are to do for Him. As you read ask yourself, 'What is God saying to me?' and remember to obey what He says to you. After you have finished the gospel of John either re-read it or go on and read the rest of the New Testament before you tackle the Old Testament.

Suggestions:

— Underline any verses that God makes especially relevant to you. This will help you find them for future use.

— Have a pad and pen available so that you can write down anything you feel God is saying to you or anything that is helpful to your relationship with God.

— Memorise verses that are meaningful to you, especially the promises of God to us as believers.

— Don't struggle with too hard to understand verses. The Lord will show you the meaning eventually. You can also ask those in your local church for help.

— Your local church will probably have either house groups or a mid-week Bible Study. It will be helpful to you if you join these so as to increase your knowledge of God's Word.

— Daily Bible reading aids are available to help you read and understand the Bible. Ask your local church for details.

Getting direction

The Christian life is like a journey and God's Word is described as,

"A lamp to my feet and a light for my path."
(Psalm 119:105)

God will speak to us and guide us if we read and meditate on His Word (the Bible). The Bible is our makers handbook. It gives us instructions and helps us understand both God who created us and also who we truly are as individuals. The Bible also shows us how to please God in every area of our life and how best we can serve Him. We should therefore, take time to read and study it.

"The entrance of your word gives light; it gives understanding to the simple." (Psalm 119:130)

What can the Word of God do?

The word of God can help us to overcome problems and confusions. It shows us how things really are because it is the truth of God revealed to us. You can trust the Scriptures.

"All Scripture is God-breathed and is useful for teaching, rebuking, correcting and training in righteousness, so that the man of God may be thoroughly equipped for every good work." (II Timothy 3:16,17)

The Word of God gives us food which will prepare us for eternity with God. It is our standard to measure the things of life against in order to assess whether they are of God and for God or not.

Can we trust the New Testament?

The following table shows the authenticity and reliability of the gospels compared with comparable secular literature.

ANCIENT WRITING	THE HISTORY of THEOYDIDES	CAESAR'S GALLIC WAR	TACITUS HISTORIES	THE FOUR GOSPELS
A. Original Document Writers	460—400 B.C.	58—50 B.C.	Approx. A.D. 100	A.D. 65-90
B. Oldest Surviving Copy	A.D. 900 (+ a few 1st Century fragments)	A.D.850	A.D.800	A.D. 350 (even earlier for fragments)
C. Approx. time between A. and B.	1,300 years (fragments 400 years)	900 years	700 years	300 years (fragments 50 years)
D. Number of current copies in existence today	8	10	4	Up to 2,000

It must be remembered that between 250-500 eye witnesses
to the resurrection of Jesus were alive when Paul and other
New Testament writers wrote their manuscripts. If the early
church writings were false then there would undoubtedly be
evidence of challenges to their authenticity, and this is not the
case. Secular writings of the time mention Jesus and do not
contradict the four gospels. Also no archaeological discovery
has cast any doubt on the truth of the Bible. These things all
point to the reliability of the New Testament.

Questions and Tips:

1. What four things does II Timothy 3:16,17 tell us the Scripture is useful for and what is God's aim in this?
2. Read Joshua 1:7,8 and then answer the following:

    a. Should we bother to read God's Word or rather just rely on what we think is right?

    b. Should we only think about God's Word occasionally when we have the time?

    c. Does God's Word actually relate to our daily lives, i.e. is it practical to help us to live?

    d. What should happen as a direct result of meditating on God's Word?

3. What can the Scriptures do for you? (II Timothy 3:15)

4. What makes the Bible different from any other book? (I Thessalonians 2:13)

5. What will happen as we hold onto the teaching of Jesus as revealed in the Bible? (John 8:31,32)

6. What are we to let the Word of God (or the Word of Christ) do? (Colossians 3:16; Romans 15:4)

7. Jesus said, "Man shall not live by bread alone" so how else should we be fed and sustained? (Matthew 4:4)

8. How is the Word of God described? (Hebrews 4:12)

9. What does the Lord want us to do and what will be the result? (Psalm 1:1-3)

Prayer:

Almighty God, I thank you that you have given us the Bible which is the Word of God revealed to us. I realise that I know so little about you and your plans for me and I want to know more. Help me to set aside time each day to read your Word, the Bible, and as I read it enable me to learn more about you and what you want me to do for you. I pray this in Jesus' name. Amen.

Study 5

Prayer: Two-Way Communication

Why do we Pray?

Prayer is simply talking with and listening to God. We need to set aside time in each day to seek God and pray to Him. This will enable our relationship with God to develop because we will be spending time communicating with Him. God wants us to talk to Him. He wants us to ask for His help and He wants to speak to us. God loves us and cares for us. In fact, He has promised never to leave us or forsake us (see Hebrews 13:5). As your relationship with God grows through your prayer life you will wonder how you ever managed before without Him.

Where does Jesus fit in?

The Son of God, Jesus, was a man just like us, and He went through all the same problems and temptations that we do. Therefore, He does understand what we need (see Hebrews 4:15). He is also now at God's right hand interceding (or praying) for us (see Romans 8:34). Jesus wants to be a friend to us and help us to live in a way that is pleasing to God. Wherever we go Jesus goes with us by the Holy Spirit. He is always there to pray to for guidance and help. We can share

our problems, our joys, and in fact, every aspect of our lives
with Him. We are now God's children and co-heirs with Jesus
(see Romans 8:17).

How should we pray?

As new Christians God knows that we have very little
knowledge of Him and He wants to help us. He will be
pleased if we simply pray to Him and ask Him for things
that we need. However, we need to grow beyond this and
begin to pray for other people and situations (see Ephesians
6:18). God eventually wants us to learn how to be directed
and led by the Holy Spirit in our praying. The Holy Spirit
is our guide and counsellor (see John 14:16, 26) and He will
teach us how to pray (see Romans 8:26,27). God not only
hears and answers our prayers; He helps us to pray them!
The Bible urges us to,

> *"Devote yourselves to prayer; being watchful and
> thankful."*   (Colossians 4:2)

In fact, we should,

> *"not be anxious about anything, but in everything, by
> prayer and petition, with thanksgiving, present your
> requests to God."*   (Philippians 4:6)

This verse also points out that as part of our prayer life we
should be thanking God for all He has done and especially
for prayer that has been answered.

Right motivation

When you pray, do it to please God and not just to please
yourself. In James 4:3 we read,

> *"When you ask, you do not receive, because you ask with wrong motives, that you may spend what you get on your pleasures."*

God wants us to pray with the right motivation. It doesn't matter if we pray hesitatingly or with faltering words. God will still hear us and act if we have the right motives. We certainly don't need to use a special religious language when we pray, and we do not have to use special prepared prayers (see John 16:24). To check your motives ask yourself whether what you pray is for God's glory and the extension of His Kingdom.

Pray with a clean heart

When we pray we need to be clean before God so that we can come before Him with confidence and look Him in the eye (see Hebrews 4:16). If you have sinned then confess your sin and ask God to forgive you (see I John 1:9). God also tells us to forgive others no matter how wrong they are, because He forgave us so much in Jesus (see Matthew 6:14,15). Once we have done this we can come before God with confidence, because we will no longer have hearts that condemn us. If we live as God wants and obey Him, we can ask and receive anything (see I John 3:21-24).

Should we pray with others?

> *"For where two or three come together in my name, there am I with them."* (Matthew 18:20)

We should pray to God alone on a daily basis. However, the Bible also mentions groups of Christians praying together to great effect (see Acts 4:23,24; 12:12). Ask your local church for details of their prayer meetings.

Prayer Suggestions:

— Prayer can be accompanied by a daily Bible reading.
— You should spend at least five minutes praying each day. As your relationship with God grows you will find that five minutes of prayer is not enough. You will want to go to God in every situation because you will only want to do His will.
— You should find somewhere for your prayer time that is quiet and where you will not be disturbed.
— In our times of prayer we should leave room for God to speak to us.
— We should pray to God the Father in Jesus' name. This helps us to keep our motivations for prayer correct and also the Bible teaches us to pray this way (see John 14:13; 16:23).
— Within our prayers it is good to praise God for who He is and to thank God for what He has done for us and others.

Questions and Tips:

1. Read Mark 11:22-25 and then answer the following questions:
     a. Who do these verses apply to?
     b. What can we do through prayer?
     c. What should be the attitude of our heart when we pray?
     d. What should we do before we pray?
2. What will you receive in prayer if you believe? (Matthew 21:21,22)
3. How may we be certain that God hears our prayers? (I John 5:14,15)
4. To what extent is God able to answer our prayers? (Ephesians 3:20)

5. What simple failure can often be the reason for us not receiving from God? (James 4:2)

6. How should I respond when I feel that I am praying according to God's will and yet my prayers seem to be unanswered? (Hebrews 10:35,36)

7. What sorts of things can we pray for? (Matthew 9:38; I Timothy 2:1,2; James 1:5)

8. Read Matthew 6:5-15 which is a passage where Jesus teaches His disciples how to pray and then answer the following questions:
   a. Where should we pray? (verse 6)
   b. Are long prayers necessary? (verse 7,8)
   c. Does God know our needs? (verse 8)
   d. To whom should we pray? (verse 9)
   e. When we pray should we exalt and lift up our Father in heaven? (verse 9)
   f. Does God want us to ask for our daily needs? (verse 11)
   g. Should we ask God to forgive us for our sins? (verse 12)
   h. Should we ask God for help to resist satan and temptation? (verse 13)
   i. Should we forgive others? (verse 14,15)

Prayer:

Almighty God, thank you for making yourself known to me. I want to get to know you more and for the relationship between us to grow. Help me to learn how to pray to you and to be disciplined in the setting aside of my time to do this. I ask this in Jesus' name. Amen.

Study 6

Fellowship With Other Christians

Fatherhood and adoption

When we accept Jesus as our Lord and Saviour we become part of God's family. God actually becomes a true Father to us and he adopts us as His son (see Galatians 3:26,27; 4:6,7). We did not deserve this and we certainly were not naturally born to it. God did it only because of Jesus. It doesn't matter whether we are male or female, God still regards us now, in Christ, as His sons. We are very precious to Him and He loves us as a true Father should (see Romans 8:38,39). He guides us, provides for us, strengthens us and helps us to live in the best possible way for our long term good. He knows what we can cope with at any particular time and He knows when we need to be disciplined (see Hebrews 12:5-11). In fact, He only allows things to happen to us for our good if we are walking in obedience to Him (Romans 8:28). He even wants us to come boldly into His presence and for us to have fellowship with Him (see Ephesians 3:12).

We need each other

As part of God's family we cannot be Christians by ourselves. God has always called His people to live in a special relationship both with Himself and with each other. We should be like coals glowing in a fire. Together, we all give warmth and light to each other as well as to others outside the fire. But if we do not get fellowship with other Christians we will begin to lose our fire—we will begin to go cold. We need to get in the fire together with other followers of Jesus. The best place to do this is in a church where Jesus Christ is preached as Saviour and Lord. Remember, the church is not the building but rather the community of people who follow Jesus. As a new Christian you need to be taught from God's Word and you need the encouragement of other people who believe the same way as you do.

God knows you

God has not chosen you by chance. He knew you before you were born and He knows where you will be best able to serve Him and learn from Him.

> *"For you created my inmost being; you knit me together in my mother's womb. I praise you because I am fearfully and wonderfully made; your works are wonderful, I know that full well. My frame was not hidden from you when I was made in the secret place. When I was woven together in the depths of the earth, your eyes saw my unformed body. All the days ordained for me were written in your book before one of them came to be."*
>
> (Psalm 139:13-16)

The church God places you in will need you as much as you need it. God has chosen you to do a specific work for Him. You are the best person for that job, so throw yourself into what you know God wants you to do. Be a worker in God's house, not a passenger. Do the little things that you see need to be done, if you have nothing else to do. Serving the church is serving God. At the beginning of your Christian life, God will probably only ask you to do small simple things. As you prove faithful in these things He will take you on to bigger and better things. He knows what you can handle.

We need the Church

The church of Jesus Christ is made up of every true Christian in the world. Obviously, all its members cannot meet at one time, so God has split up His worldwide church into local areas. These are the local churches which we, as part of the family of God, need to attend. God instituted these local churches to enable Christians to:—

— have fellowship with each other
— grow spiritually
— worship God
— serve God
— and reach out to the world with the message of God's salvation in Jesus.

"Let us not give up meeting together, as some are in the habit of doing, but let us encourage one another—and all the more as you see the Day approaching."

(Hebrews 10:25)

Part of a body

The church of Jesus Christ is described in the Bible as the body of Christ (see Ephesians 1:22,23). Just as a human body only functions as a whole—its members never do their own thing—so it should be with the church. The members of the church of Jesus Christ belong to one another (see Ephesians 4:25) and they are all important. In fact, every part needs to function (see Ephesians 4:16). It follows that we as individuals need to be vitally involved in the body of Christ locally.

Worship in the church

When the church meets together, it is important to recognise that we should give time for worshipping God. We worship God not only for what He has done for us or through us, but for who He is. We are encouraged to join in this worship by contributing a hymn (or chorus), a word of instruction, a revelation, a tongue, or an interpretation, so that the church may be strengthened (see I Corinthians 14:26).

It's the people that count

When we as Christians meet together, the building isn't the important thing, it is the people that count.

Jesus said,

> *"For where two or three come together in my name, there am I with them."*   (Matthew 18:20)

We are no longer aliens to God but rather we are members of God's household with Jesus at the centre of us all. In Jesus we are all joined and built together to become a place where God lives by His Spirit (see Ephesians 2:19-22). Share your faith with others in the body of Christ (the church) and let them share their faith with you.

Questions and Tips:

1. Read Hebrews 10:23-25 and answer the following questions:
   a. Is God faithful? (verse 23)

      b. Should we spur one another on and to what? (verse 24)

      c. Is church attendance optional? (verse 25)

2. Have all Christians in the local church (or body of Christ) an important part to play in its life? (Romans 12:3-8)

3. How should the believer regard his fellow believers? (Philippians 2:3)

4. What was Paul's desire for the early churches? (I Corinthians 1:10)

5. Why is it necessary for believers to be united? (Romans 15:5,6; John 17:20-23)

6. How should we respond to leaders in the church? (Hebrews 13:7)

7. What can you do for God in your local church?

8. Read I Corinthians 12:12-27 and answer the following:

      a. What is the church likened to in this passage?

      b What kinds of things are the individual Christians in the church likened to?

      c. Are we all created to function the same way or differently?

      d. Do we decide what part we should play in the church? If not, who does?

      e. Would the church function as it should, if we did nothing or just what we wanted rather than follow God?

      f. Are we equally important in the church whatever part we play?

Prayer:

Almighty God, I thank you for placing me into your family. I ask you to show me clearly which local expression of your worldwide family you want me to join. I recognise the need I have to relate to my fellow believers. I also ask you to give me lasting friendships within the local church in which you place me. I am willing to serve that part of the body of Christ in any way that you ask of me because I know that as I serve the church, I serve you. I ask this in Jesus' precious name. Amen.

Study 7

Spirit, Soul And Body

Man is spirit, soul and body. We need to understand the function of each of these parts of our person and how they relate to each other.

The Human Spirit

> *"Flesh gives birth to flesh, but Spirit gives birth to spirit."*
> (John 3:6)

As we are born in the flesh, our human spirit is, to all intents and purposes, useless. It is inactive because we are spiritually dead; we do not have communion or fellowship with God. Our human spirit is not alive, because we have not been 'born of the Spirit'.

> *Jesus said, "Unless a man is born again, he cannot see the kingdom of God."* (John 3:3)

Our spirit does not exercise any real influence upon us until this spiritual rebirth takes place. Then we can know God for ourselves, we are able to hear Him and speak to Him personally. Our body becomes the temple of the Holy Spirit because God has come to live in us. Our spirit, therefore, can be defined as the God awareness (God conscious) part of us or the place within us in which the Holy Spirit is able to reside.

The Soul

The soul consists of 3 main areas of our life:

    a. The Mind—our thinking and intellectual process.
    b. The Emotions—our affections and feelings.
    c. The Will—our ability to choose and determine what we do.

The word Jesus used in His teaching can be translated either 'soul' or 'life'. The soul is the non-physical part of the natural man, the person that he is, his personality and character. Until we are born again of the Spirit of God, our soul will run our life. We are used to assessing situations with our mind and reaching our own conclusions and we pay a lot of attention to our emotions and very often allow them to rule us.

The Body

The physical body houses the soul and the spirit. Whatever goes on in our soul determines what we do in the body. Our body reacts to the thoughts of our mind, it expresses the emotions and responds to the decisions of the will.

When we are born again our body becomes the dwelling place or temple of the Holy Spirit. This means that we can live under the direction of the Spirit of God. He breathes life into our human spirit and the whole direction and influence of our life is altered. Now, instead of being under the domination of our soul and body with all their negative power and influences, we can know God's power working in us as He touches our spirit by His Spirit.

Our spirit can begin, therefore, to exercise its proper control over the soul, informing the mind, emotions and will of God's purpose. The body can then be directed by the Spirit working through the soul, to accomplish the will and purpose of God.

*"Therefore, if anyone is in Christ, he is a new creation;
the old has gone, the new has come!"*

(II Corinthians 5:17)

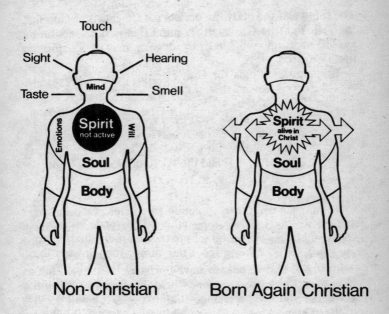

Non-Christian   Born Again Christian

The Renewal of your Mind

The five senses (i.e. touch, taste, sight, smell and hearing)
all feed into the mind and are processed there like a computer.
We begin to think and act according to what we input into
our minds. The Bible encourages us to no longer feed into
our minds as the world does but rather to have a change of
input and therefore to allow the renewing of our mind.

"Do not conform any longer to the pattern of this world, but be transformed by the renewing of your mind."

(Romans 12:2)

The mind and the body are outlets for the Spirit of God that indwells the true Christian. A mind that is not functioning as God wants it to will hinder the development of our spiritual life. We need to:

— Prepare our minds for God's action (see I Peter 1:13).
— Take captive every thought to make it obedient to Christ (see II Corinthians 10:5).
— Make sure our minds aren't led astray from our sincere and pure devotion to Christ Jesus (see II Corinthians 11:3).
— Occupy our minds with godly thoughts (see Philippians 4:8,9; Titus 2:11-14) and the Word of God (see Hebrews 4:12, 13; II Timothy 3: 16, 17).

In fact, we need to completely surrender our minds and actions over to God (see Romans 12:1). The Holy Spirit living within us wants to show us God's way to live. We must choose whether we will obey Him or do what we ourselves want to do. Our minds, as new Christians, tend to think as they used to before knowing Christ Jesus. Now you are a Christian you need a change in thinking. This will require discipline and time. As you yield more of your mind over to God's leading and less to you old desires and what your five senses tell you to do, then the more your mind will be as God wants it to be.

Spirit of God	←———— Mind ————→	5 Senses, our old
through our		way of thinking,
spirit		and satan

Questions and Tips:

1. Does our mind need to be changed? (Romans 8:5-7; Ephesians 2:3; 4:17,18)
2. Can you think of anything that you do or often think about that needs to change?
3. Will God help you to change? (I Thessalonians 5:23,24)
4. Is it important to yield our life to the control of God's Holy Spirit? (Romans 8:12-14; I Corinthians 2:9-16)

Prayer:

Almighty God, I thank you that you have made my spirit alive with your Holy Spirit. I know that I have much that needs to change in the way I think and in what I do. I give my life over into the control of your Holy Spirit who dwells in me. Change me as you know I need to be changed so that I may serve you better and live as you want me to live. Make me as you want me to be in body, soul and spirit. I ask this in Jesus' precious name. Amen.

Study 8

The Power of the Holy Spirit

Who is the Holy Spirit?

The Holy Spirit is God. There is one God who has three parts:

God the Father, God the Son (Jesus) and God the Holy Spirit

To help you see how how this is possible consider an apple. It has a skin, the flesh and a core. One apple with three parts. The Holy Spirit is a person, not a force or a vague mist-like influence. We should always refer to the Holy Spirit as 'He' and not 'it'.

"If you love me, you will obey what I command. And I will ask the Father, and he will give you another Counsellor to be with you for ever—the Spirit of truth. The world cannot accept him, because it neither sees him nor knows him. But you know him, for he lives with you and will be in you."   (John 14:15-17)

Why do we need the Holy Spirit?

1. The Holy Spirit will show us our sinful state and our need of God. (see John 16:7-11)

2. He will also enable us to be born into God's family by making our spirits alive to God when we are born again. (see John 3:5-8; II Corinthians 3:6).

3. Jesus wanted His work continued in the world after He had died, was resurrected and He went to be with His Father in heaven. Jesus Himself did not start His work on earth until He had received the Holy Spirit (see Luke 3:21-23).

   He needed to be filled with the Holy Spirit to empower Him to do all the work that God had asked Him to do. Jesus told those whom He trained to continue His work, that they also needed the same power to do this work. They were to wait until they were clothed with power from on high, that is, be filled or baptised with the Holy Spirit (see Acts 1:4,5,8).

   This was a promise from God the Father that would come as a result of Jesus going to the Father and being glorified (see Luke 24:46-49; John 16:7). Being filled or baptised with the Holy Spirit is an experience whereby the believer is completely clothed with the supernatural power of the Holy Spirit to do the works of Christ and to live the Spirit—filled Christian life. It is the doorway leading from a natural realm of Christianity to a more supernatural realm of life in the Spirit.

Is this power available today?

The Holy Spirit wasn't just given to the generation after Jesus left the earth, it was a promise to all who are true Christians. This power is still available today for those who will ask. The Holy Spirit comes not only for our salvation but also to enable us to serve God more effectively and fruitfully.

> *"Repent and be baptised, every one of you, in the name of Jesus Christ so that your sins may be forgiven. And you will receive the gift of the Holy Spirit. The promise is for you and your children and for all who are far off—for all the Lord our God will call."*   (Acts 2:38,39)

What will the Holy Spirit do to me?

The Holy Spirit is not going to force you to do anything. Before we are born again into God's Kingdom we are like a marionette puppet with strings that satan has a hold of to manipulate us. After we are born again these strings are cut. God, however, does not then pick up the strings to manipulate us. He gives us His Holy Spirit and He will show us God's way if we let Him. He will not force us to do God's will. We have to decide. We are given control of ourselves by God and therefore we must choose: God's way or our own. God not only wants to guide us but also to fill us and empower us with the Holy Spirit.

How do we get filled or baptised with the Holy Spirit?

The Holy Spirit is likened to the wind (see John 3:8). No one can create or control the wind but we can put ourselves in a place where we can experience the wind when it blows. We can throw open the windows and doors to let the breeze come in and we can also do the same thing with our lives by opening them to the Holy Spirit. We need to yield every area of our lives over to God and allow Jesus to be Lord of them for us to be filled with the Holy Spirit. The Spirit of God will not come where He is not wanted or not asked or where there is sin.

Jesus said,

> *"If a man is thirsty, let him come to me and drink. Whoever believes in me, as the Scripture has said, streams of living water will flow from within him. By this he meant the Spirit, whom those who believed in him were later to receive. Up to that time the Spirit had not been given, since Jesus had not yet been glorified."*   (John 7:37-39)

Jesus also said,

> *"Ask and it will be given to you; seek and you will find; knock and the door will be opened to you. For everyone who asks receives; he who seeks finds; and to him who knocks, the door will be opened. Which of you fathers, if your son asks for a fish, will give him a snake instead? Or if he asks for an egg, will give him a scorpion? If you then, though you are evil, know how to give good gifts to your children, how much more will you Father in heaven give the Holy Spirit to those who ask Him!"*
>   (Luke 11:9-13).

What about tongues?

When you are filled with the Holy Spirit, it is quite common to find yourself speaking in another language (known as tongues) that you have not learned. There is no need to fear this. It is the Holy Spirit speaking through you to God. When you speak in tongues, the Bible says you will be edified (or built up) (see I Corinthians 14:1-5).

Are you only filled once?

When the Apostle Paul wrote "Be filled with the Spirit" in Ephesians 5:18, the tense he used implied that we should go on being filled with the Spirit. It should be a continuous, daily, ever-fresh renewing. Our lives need to be constantly open to the Spirit of God.

What does the Holy Spirit do to us?

He gives us:
1. Power to belong to Jesus Christ and the Kingdom of God (see John 3:5-8; Romans 8:9,16,17).
2. Power to live as Jesus wants us to live (see Ephesians 3:16; Romans 8:11,14).
3. Power to be witnesses for God (see Acts 1:8; I Corinthians 2:4,5).
4. Power to understand God and His ways (see Ephesians 1:17-21; I Corinthians 2:9-16; John 16:13-15).
5. Power to pray to God (see Romans 8:26,27).
6. Power to fellowship with God and other Christians (see Philippians 2:1,2).
7. Power to overcome our old sinful nature, sin, death, satan, and the world (see II Corinthians 3:17; I John 4:4; Romans 8:2; Galatians 5:16).
8. Power to love and hope (see Romans 5:5; Romans 15:13).

Questions and Tips:

1. Who will baptise or fill you with the Holy Spirit? (Mark 1:7,8)
2. What are three things the Holy Spirit will do for us? (John 14:26; 16:13)
3. What should be the result of receiving the promise of the Father? (Acts 1:8)
4. Where does the Holy Spirit choose to live (I Corinthians 3:16) and how should we live as a result? (I Corinthians 6:19,20)

5. What are the nine gifts of the Holy Spirit and who decides what each man's gift will be? (I Corinthians 12:8-11)
6. To whom are the gifts given and what is their purpose? (I Corinthians 12:7)
7. What are the nine fruits of the Holy Spirit? (Galatians 5:22,23)
8. What type of worshippers is the Father seeking? (John 4:23,24)
9. Read Galatians 5:16-18,25 and answer the following:
   a. Do the desires of the sinful nature and the Spirit lead us in the same direction?
   b. Who should we be led by?
10. What are three ways we can hinder the work of the Holy Spirit? (I Thessalonians 5:19; Ephesians 4:30; Acts 7:51)

Prayer:

Almighty God, I thank you for your precious gift of the Holy Spirit. I see my need to be filled with your gift. I ask you to forgive any sin I may have committed against you and I thank you for your forgiveness. I yield my life afresh to you. I ask you now to fill me with your Holy Spirit in order to empower me for the work you want me to do for you. Thank you Lord that you have promised to give the Holy Spirit in this way to all who ask. I pray this in Jesus' name. Amen.

Study 9

What To Watch Out For

Temptation and how to deal with it

We are born with a bias to go off course just like a lawn bowl. The Bible says our old nature is responsible for this. As a result we always turn away from the straight course set by God's Word. When we are born again and we become God's children we are still able to sin but we no longer have to. We are free to learn to achieve what God wants and not to mess it up as we did in the past. It is not necessary for a Christian to sin because God has given us the power to resist the temptation to sin.

> *"No temptation has seized you except what is common to man. And God is faithful; he will not let you be tempted beyond what you can bear. But when you are tempted, he will also provide a way out so that you can stand up under it."* (I Corinthians 10:13)

We do not have to yield to any temptation to sin because God will give us help and strength to resist and overcome if we look to Him.

What if we do sin?

Temptation to sin is not sin. Even Jesus was tempted (see Matthew 4:1-11). It is yielding to temptation that is sin. Even if we do fail, we have forgiveness available to us in Jesus. All we have to do is confess to God that we have let God down in whatever area and ask Him to forgive us and He will. God will forget we ever did wrong. Jesus was punished, judged and condemned for all sins, therefore, if we ask God for forgiveness we can forget about that sin and go on with life, clean and right before God (see I John 1:9).

Jesus can help us

> *"For we do not have a high priest (Jesus) who is unable to sympathize with our weaknesses, but we have one who has been tempted in every way, just as we are—yet without sin."*
> (Hebrews 4:15)

Jesus experienced the same temptations to sin as we do and yet He resisted them all and didn't sin once. He can help us to do the same if we give our lives over to Him.

Reap what you sow

There is a principle in God's Kingdom that is universal: You reap what you sow (see Luke 6:38). If you sow living in wilful sin and disobedience to God you will reap misery, selfishness and a sense of failure. But if you sow a life that is pleasing to God you will be fulfilled in your life on earth. This means we have to live as God wants and not as we feel we want to. God will help us to turn away from any temptation to sin if we let Him. Our rewards in heaven depend on what we do now (see I Corinthians 3:11-15).

Who is satan anyway?

Satan or the devil is a fallen angel of God who rebelled against God because of pride. He is our enemy because he stands against everything that is of God.

> *"Be self-controlled and alert. Your enemy the devil prowls around like a roaring lion looking for someone to devour. Resist him, standing firm in the faith."* (I Peter 5:8,9)

God shows us in the Bible that we need to watch out in case the devil gets a foothold in our lives (see Ephesians 4:27). The devil is not a gentleman. He wants our destruction and he will look for our weaknesses and play on them at the worst possible moments. We need to submit ourselves to God and resist the devil and he will flee from us (see James 4:7).

> *"He who does what is sinful is of the devil, because the devil has been sinning from the beginning. The reason the Son of God appeared was to destroy the devil's work."*(I (I John 3:8)

> *"Having disarmed the powers and authorities (of the devil), he (Jesus) made a public spectacle of them, triumphing over them by the Cross."* (Colossians 2:15)

The devil is real and he is your enemy. One of his most effective weapons is discouragement, so watch out for him (see II Corinthians 2:11). Remember though, Jesus did triumph over the devil and all his powers (called demons) on the Cross. We are in Jesus (see Colossians 3:3) and therefore we have been given authority also over the devil and his demons. The devil has to give way if we resist him with a clean heart before God and in the authority of the name of Jesus.

> *"You are a chosen people, a royal priesthood, a holy nation, a people belonging to God, that you may declare the praises of him who called you out of darkness into His wonderful light."* (I Peter 2:9)

Questions and Tips:

1. Do you think a Christian just stops sinning and begins to live righteously without having to do anything about it himself? (Colossians 3:5-14; Philippians 2:12,13; I John 1:8-2:2)
2. Does God ever tempt us? (James 1:13-15)
3. Where is the devil now in relation to Jesus? (Ephesians 1:19-23)
4. Will the devil (or satan) try to influence our thinking? (II Corinthians 4:4; 11:3,14)
5. Read the following verses for your encouragement: Philippians 4:13; James 1:2-4; I John 4:4.

Prayer:

Almighty God, I thank you that you have taken from me the natural bias towards sinful living. I know that I will be tempted to sin but I ask you to give me the strength to resist any temptation that comes my way. I want to follow you and please you. I recognise also that satan will attempt to cause me to fail you. I thank you that you have won a complete victory over satan and all his works in Jesus and I again submit my life to you. Having done this I know that when I resist the devil he will flee from me. I pray this in the mighty name of Jesus. Amen.

Study 10

Witnessing: Disciples In Action

Tell others about the One who saved you

As Christians we should tell others about Jesus and how they too can be born again by receiving Him into their lives. This is called witnessing.

Jesus said,

> *"All authority in heaven and on earth has been given to me. Therefore go and make disciples of all nations."*
> (Matthew 28:18,19)

If you were drowning in a nearby lake and you couldn't swim, and I dived in, pulled you out and saved your life, you would think that I was the best person on earth! You would want all your friends to know about it and you wouldn't be ashamed to introduce them to me. Jesus has saved you from something far worse than physical death. He saved you from eternal separation from God in hell. We have a responsiblity in God to reach out to other people and to tell them what God has done for us. Our friends, workmates and family, in fact, the whole world needs to know what is available to them in Jesus.

Jesus said,

> *"Go into all the world and preach the good news to all creation."*   (Mark 16:15)

Someone told you about Jesus and what He has done for you. Do not keep Him to yourself. Share Him with others.

What do I say?

Your life has been changed by Jesus. How would you explain this to somebody in simple easy to understand language? This is called giving your testimony. You also need to think about how to give a clear explanation of what you believe. The second study in this course will help you. It would be helpful to learn some relevant Bible verses. The following table gives a step by step pathway showing the way to salvation in Jesus.

God's love and salvation plan in Jesus	John 3:16
Man's sinfulness	Romans 3:23
The punishment for sin	Romans 6:23
Turning from sin (repentance)	Acts 3:19
Jesus is the answer	John 14:6
Receiving Christ	Romans 10:9,10
Assurance of salvation	John 5:24;
	I John 5:11,12

Review (ask them what they would tell a friend who wanted to become a Christian)

It is helpful to write the first Scripture in the front of your Bible so that you can find it and then underline the words in the text. Write the next Scripture in the pathway at the bottom of that page so that you will also know where it is found. You can then progress right through the pathway. However, the best method is to memorise either these Scriptures or find your own to memorise.

Peter wrote,

> *"Always be prepared to give an answer to everyone who asks you to give the reason for the hope that you have."*
> (I Peter 3:15)

As someone who has experienced God's saving love, you have much to share. Remember though, when you tell someone about Jesus, to keep it simple and avoid confusing the person. Stick to the basic facts by telling them about Jesus, His love and what He has done for you and them.

A pattern for witnessing

Jesus gave a good pattern for witnessing in John 4:7-26. He opened the conversation, written about in this Bible passage, with a subject familiar to the woman He was talking to. He then turned the conversation to spiritual things. He brought her to recognise the fact of her sin. He revealed Himself as the Christ and showed her that He was able to meet her need. We can use a similar approach but instead of pointing people to ourselves, we can point them to Jesus.

Prayer

Another thing we can do is to pray to God for our family and friends, that God may reveal Himself to them also and convince them of their need to accept Jesus as their Lord and Saviour. List the names of friends and relatives and begin praying for them on a regular basis. You will be amazed at what God will do.

Be sensitive

There will be a time, a place and a way to witness for Jesus. Ask God to show you and to provide the opportunities. It is no good nagging someone into submission or making a continual nuisance of yourself. The best way to witness is to show others that Jesus has made a lasting consistent change in your life and let that speak for itself. Other people with whom you are in contact will probably then come and ask you what has happened. Be ready with an explanation.

You may be mocked, so what!

You may be laughed at, called names or mocked for what you say, so what! Men did far worse to Jesus and He could have done something about it. He didn't retaliate because He came to die and to suffer for you and for me. We have got the greatest possession that anyone can have: friendship with God. It is far better to have God's favour and blessing by doing what He asks than the favour of other people who are one day going to fade away and perish.
Jesus said,

> *"Whoever serves me must follow me; and where I am, my servant also will be. My Father will honour the one who serves me."*   (John 12:26)

Questions and Tips:

1. What is necessary before people can call upon the Lord Jesus and believe in Him for their salvation? (Romans 10:13-15)
2. What responsibility have we for bringing men to Christ? (II Corinthians 5:18-21)

3. For what should we pray as we witness for Christ? (Acts 1:8; 4:29-31; Colossians 4:3)
4. Why should we continue to witness fearlessly? (Romans 1:16)
5. Can we show Jesus to other people by our life? (Matthew 5:13-16)
6. When will Jesus acknowledge us before our Father in heaven? (Matthew 10:32)
7. Write down your testimony using no more than one page.
8. How would you answer the following questions:
   a. What more can God expect of me than doing good and helping others? (Ephesians 2:8,9 ; Titus 3:5)
   b. Don't all religions lead to the same place? (John 14:6)
   c. I have never done anything very wrong! (John 3:3; Romans 3:23)
   d. I intend to follow Jesus later in life. (II Corinthians 6:2; James 4:14)

Prayer:

Almighty God, I thank You for all that You have already done for me in Jesus. You have given me Your love and a hope and I praise You that You have accepted me as Your child. Lord, help me to be a witness for You as I know I should be. Show me the people I need to pray for and those I should speak to about You. I want as many people as possible to know You as I do. Help me also to live a life that is pleasing to You so that other people can see You in me. Lord Jesus, You started the work and You commissioned us to go on and to complete it, making disciples of all nations. Lord I offer myself up for You to use in this task. Here am I Lord, send me. I ask this in Jesus' name and for His glory, Amen.

GLOSSARY

Advocate: is one who comes alongside of us and speaks on
  our behalf or helps us in our time of need.

Assurance: being sure about something or being entirely
  confident.

Atonement: to pay the penalty of or make amends for man's
  sin by the sacrifice of the Lord Jesus Christ when He
  shed His blood and died on the Cross.

Baptised: means to totally immerse or be filled.

Christians: are also called saints, believers or disciples.

Church: is the same as saying the body of Christ or just the
  body and it usually speaks of a community or group
  of Christians rather than a church building.

Conviction: is when we realise that we are in error or we
  realise that we are sinners and are separated from God
  and condemned (found guilty).

Disciple: is a follower or an adherent. They learn from the
  one they follow usually by obeying their teachings and
  imitating them.

Faith: is believing in God and His Word rather than what
  we see or feel.

Fellowship: is a sharing in common or communion.

Gospel: means good news.

Grace: is God's Riches At Christ's Expense. It is something
  we don't deserve but God has made available to us
  anyway in Jesus.

Justification: is God looking at us in Jesus and it is JUST
  as IF we have never sinned.

Prayer: is simply talking to and listening to God.

Redemption: means to release on payment of a ransom or
  to buy out (especially of purchasing a slave with a view
  to his freedom).

Repentance: is to turn 180° or to have another mind.

Righteousness: is the character or quality of being right or just.

Salvation: means deliverance or preservation. This word is used mainly to refer to the spiritual and eternal deliverance granted immediately by God to those who accept His conditions of repentance and faith in the Lord Jesus Christ.

Saved: means to be born again into God's Kingdom or become a true Christian.

Saviour: is a deliverer or preserver.

Sinful nature: is our nature that tends towards sin all the time and over which we had no real control until we became a Christian.

Word of God: is the Scriptures (the Bible) or in general terms, it refers to Words spoken by God.

Finally!

If you have any questions arising from this booklet, general questions relating to what you have done when you accepted Jesus as your Lord and Saviour, and became a disciple of Jesus, OR if you have any difficulty finding a good church to attend, please write to:

A teaching manual entitled 'The Foundations of Christian Living' is also available, explaining in far more depth what it means to be a disciple of Jesus. It is designed both for individual and group study and is available from:

Sovereign World
PO Box 17
Chichester
West Sussex
PO20 6RY